You're In!

College Planning for High School Students

Expert advice from a college admission professional. This is a practical guide to college acceptance. Learn how to choose a college, what a college admissions committee looks for in the application and what you can do to secure your admissions.

Deborah Battle Pointer, M.Ed

To my amazing daughter, Robin Pointer and the Whalley family, in gratitude for your support and encouragement throughout this project. And, to all the first-generation college students who were raised by their grandparents like myself and became the first generation in their family to go to college. I want to encourage you, no matter how hard it gets, you can go to college.

Contents

Introduction

So, you are not a legacy, your parents or grandparents did not attend college. You will be the first in your family to go to college. Your parents are not rich, so they will not have the money to endow a faculty chair or build a campus building to influence your application. Nor are you politically connected, no Senator, Congressman or United States President will be writing a letter or making a phone call to the college on your behalf.

But Yes, You Can Still Go to College

If you are a high school senior, or the parent of one, you are about to experience a year that may be the most academically challenging, the most anxiety-ridden and the most exciting in your life. Deciding which college to apply to is both intimidating and hard work. You also face the challenge of transitioning from high school to college, deciding whether to commute to college or live on campus, and how you will pay for your education.

You have always dreamed about this day. You may be the first one in your family to attend college and your family's hopes and dreams are with you. But now, with the economy in flux and worldwide financial issues, you are wondering whether or not you can afford the cost of college. These are challenging times; many families are loosing their homes to foreclosure; thousands of people are laid off from their jobs with factories and plants moving overseas and your parents may be worried about their retirement. Recent college graduates are complaining about their high amount of college debt. Yes, you want to go to college but you don't want to put a financial burden on your family or on your future.

The good news is that if you plan carefully, you can do it, you can get accepted to college and you can find a way to afford it. With good planning and hard work, you can develop strategies to get accepted to college and to find the financial aid you may need. Education is a lifetime commitment and an investment of time and money. Yes, you can go to college, but you must plan and choose wisely.

Even with college tuition rising, the sticker price is usually not what you have to pay when you attend college. The bottom line is, the average cost of college is far below the cost of the most expensive colleges. In fact, the most aid available to help students is often given out by the most expensive universities. Few colleges charge students the real cost of a college education.

Student financial aid is available from a number of sources including the Federal government, State government, colleges and universities and other organizations. Some students receive scholarships for outstanding achievements, athletic skill, special talents or academic merit. Others receive financial aid based on financial need. So, choose a school carefully. The choice of an educational program and the college you attend can be critical in helping you prepare for gainful employment after graduation.

Be honest with yourself about your college preferences. Make sure that the colleges you choose to apply to are what you want and not just your best friend's choices. Narrow your list and try to visit the colleges that really interest you. College visits are the best way to see if you would enjoy studying on a campus. If it's too far to visit the colleges you are interested in, or you can't afford to make a visit, you can see many campuses on the web. But you have to get started now.

You're In?

It's o.k. You are in twelfth grade and haven't begun the college admissions process. In fact, you haven't done anything yet and you are starting to panic. Your friends are telling you what colleges they are applying to, they have scheduled college interviews and have even begun to draft their college essays. Some are paying thousand of dollars to college admission coaches which you could never afford. So, you might start to panic right? You haven't even written to one college for an application. Thank God you took the standardized ACT or SAT in 11th grade or maybe you didn't.

You know that you should take the exams again, but you didn't sign up. And then there's your mother panicking with you in the background. What are you going to do? How are you going to survive all this college business as well as do your school work? Don't choke; don't panic, there is still time. Yes, you can do it, but you have to start right now. Let's go!

Did You Ever Ask Yourself the Question: Why Do Some Kids Get into College and Others Do Not?

I know you have. You've heard of the horror stories buzzing around your high school about the student that didn't get accepted anywhere. You know, the girl with the perfect SAT scores that got waitlisted at a prestigious school. Or the class valedictorian with a high GPA but took no honors or AP classes, applied to a competitive school because of her GPA and was rejected.

Can you imagine being the only one in your senior class that wasn't accepted into a college?

What do you tell your friends and family? Can you imagine the embarrassment? Can you hear your mother buzzing in your ear, "I told you so?" Is the college application process and choosing a college a game of chance or one of strategy?

I know that you are hoping and praying that you are not the student this year that has nothing to announce at senior assembly. But that still doesn't answer the question, why do some kids get into college and others do not?

Think about it. Every year thousands of students wonder if they will be accepted into college. Did they get the little envelope, the big envelope or the mailing tube or e-mail filled with "Congratulations" and confetti? Or were they like you, starting late and hoping and praying that they do everything right. I know that choosing the right college is a big decision for you and your entire family. Education is a lifetime investment of time, money and effort.

Yet the college search is an intimidating process for most families. Will you get accepted? Can you afford it? Do you have to be lucky, a legacy or have lots of money to get into college? Must you be a straight "A" student?

Every year you hear of bright high school students who don't get accepted into any college. Recently, the niece of my neighbor was one of those students. She applied to two colleges and didn't get accepted anywhere. Didn't get accepted anywhere!

She is a pretty good student, with decent SAT scores and lots of extracurricular activities. But she didn't get accepted anywhere. There are thousands of colleges to choose from. There must have been one right for her. Why she was not accepted? What happened?

Is it that...

Her grades were not good enough
Her SAT or ACT scores were too low
She wrote poor essays
Her recommendation letters weren't strong
She had a bad interview

The College Admissions Process is Extremely Competitive

Just ask yourself the question, what was the difference between the students that did not get accepted and the ones that did? What was different about those applicants? What gave them a competitive edge? What made their college application stand out? What was the **college admissions success factor**? Planning.

Will Your College Admissions Counselor Help?

Of course. Start today. Even though it's your senior year you need to make an appointment with you high school college counselor **right away** so that you know the deadlines that your school may have established for the college admission process. Usually, they want all of your materials in the guidance office by mid or late November in order to help you.

Let's face it, most high school guidance counselors don't have the time to give you the personalized attention that you may need because they are working with so many students. That's why you can't wait until the last minute.

This little book will give you the competitive edge in the admissions process. You will get much closer to your goals and achieve success. I guarantee you that if you do everything that I suggest you will have some choices to make after your senior year of high school.

Let me ask you – if you were a basketball enthusiast and you had the opportunity to have **Michael Jordan** give you one-on-one personal basketball coaching, would your game improve? Your game would improve greatly right? So, you've got your own personal coach, this little book. I promise you that if you do all the things that I suggest to you, you will be successful. Are you ready?

Do You Want to Become a Master of Your College Admissions Process?

If we work together, and you follow my direction, you will be off to a good start. You must commit to putting the guidance to work, to follow the schedule and to work hard. If you plan early, submit paperwork on time and meet all deadlines, you will be successful. So, let me ask you, are you ready to start your college admissions process. I promise that if you read this book you will know that **successful college admissions is not a secret.**

Now take a minute, close your eyes and imagine yourself walking down the aisle in cap and gown from your favorite university. You stand proud, filled with pride and happy for their accomplishments as you receive their diploma. You have done it. You are successful, a college graduate.

Are you ready? Let me help make the dream of a college degree a reality for you. I will give you everything you need to be successful. You may jump around in this book to meet your current needs or questions that you might have at a particular moment. I suggest that you read this book through its entirety at least once.

Getting Started: Let's Create Your Goal

What is your goal? Is it: **Getting accepted to the college of your choice**. Write it down in a short concise, statement. Read it aloud to yourself at least three times a day. Commit yourself to giving your time and your resources to reaching your goal. Also, share your goal with someone who will understand and believe in what you are doing. Don't share your goal with a friend or associate who will make fun of your goal or discourage you. You want someone in your corner who will encourage you as well as provide knowledge and constructive criticism. Select someone who will help you reach your goal.

Ask yourself is your goal realistic? If your goal is to get accepted to Harvard and you have a 2.0 grade point average, is that realistic? You need to select colleges that you will be applying to that are based on where you are right now. Be realistic in setting your goal. Are you ready for a four-year college? Perhaps you should begin your college career at a community college building up your grade point average (GPA) and demonstrating that you can do college level work, you can always choose a community college that has articulation agreements with four-year colleges that guarantees your admissions.

Is your goal flexible? There are many factors that will affect your college decision, like your grade point average and finances. Maybe you have to start at a local community college because your grades aren't great and you need to build a great grade point average before you transfer to a four-year college. Or maybe financially you can't afford a four-year school right now and need to build up some cash reserves. Maybe you will be working while attending a local community college. Whatever is going on right now with you, know that you can change your situation if you put your mind and heart to it.

Remember, you can always transfer later (if your grades are good) to the four-year school and your bachelor's degree will only state the college that you graduated from. And, if it is a financial issue, staying close to home gives you the opportunity to save money and to make choices about your future academic decision.

Be specific when you write down your goal. The goal that you write down should be definite and specific. Your goal should be measurable: To get accepted to the college of my choice by the end of my senior year.

Set a definite time period for you to reach your goal. That means that you have to pay close attention to college application deadlines and complete all parts of your application in a timely way. You can have all of the best intentions but if you miss the college application deadline dates it means nothing. Some schools receive so many applications that they don't even consider late applications no matter how good you are.

See your goal completed in your vision for your future. What's your career goal? Do you want to be a doctor, lawyer, actor or basketball star? See yourself in the career which you are preparing for when you are in undergraduate college. You know that if you want to be a doctor you have to go to medical school after college, or if you want to be a lawyer you have to go to law school. Even a basketball star is usually drafted while in college or after graduating from college; very few basketball stars are recruited right out of high school. Even actors study acting before landing a role and/or getting an agent to help them get the starring role in a movie. But you have to get started. You have to see yourself at the beginning and at the end of your goal. Set goals that reflect your vision.

Senior Year Timeline for Success

So, let's get started, let's look at college admissions.

In order to get started answer the questions listed below. These questions will jump start your college applications process. Your answer may surprise you. And, you might find out that you have more than one answer a question. Let's do a personal assessment.

Please note that the first question is one of the most important:

So, Why Do You Really Want to Go to College?

Take a realistic look at your self, what are your strengths and what are your weaknesses?
What are your goals? What is it that you expect to accomplish during your college experience and how does your college going affect future goals for your life?

Are you really ready? Are you ready to make an academic commitment to college? College is expensive; so, you don't want to waste your time or money. Will you be ready to go right after high school or should you work a year, or travel abroad to get more focused before you go to college?

Are you mature enough to attend a college far from home? Or, do you want to attend a college close to home? In what type of college environment would you feel most comfortable?

Can you and your family afford college? What can you afford? Do you need financial assistance?

Getting Started

1. Make your college list. If you follow the questions in the next section: **Finding the Right College**, you will know what questions to ask as you make your list. There are many excellent directories to help you search for colleges:

ARCO, the Right College
Barron's Profile of American Colleges
Lovejoy's College Guide
The College Blue Book
Fiske Guide to Colleges
Insiders Guide to Colleges

Or you can go online and search:
www.collegeboard.org
www.petersons.com

Talk to your family, friends and teachers. Ask them to tell you about the colleges that they like. Then do your homework, ask yourself the important questions and see if some of the colleges that they represented to you are a good fit for you.

Finding the Right College

Getting into college, and choosing the right college to apply to, is not a mystery. But it does seem overwhelming unless you have a plan. A plan that gives you a roadmap and strategy to choosing the right colleges to apply to.

But how do you do that? There are almost four thousand colleges to apply to. How do you narrow your college search down to just three or ten colleges? Since you know that you want to go to college, how do you find the right one, the college that is the perfect fit for you? What type of school feels right to you, a small liberal arts college or a big university?

Every year there are students who do not get accepted into any college. That's because they did not know how to find the right colleges to apply to. They did not have a sound plan or strategy when they made their college application list. One student I know only applied to one college. When that college said no, the student had to scramble to get accepted somewhere. So how do you make your list?

Choosing the right college is a big decision for your entire family. Education is a lifetime investment of time, money and effort. This is a tough and important decision.

First, you must ask yourself some important questions. If you don't ask yourself these questions now, you may be asking yourself the same questions as a freshman looking at finding a college to transfer to. Don't apply to a college simply because your best friend applied there or it's a prestigious school. If you don't ask yourself the right questions concerning what is important to you, you might choose the wrong college. The following is a list of questions that you should ask yourself as you are building your college list:

<u>Location</u> – Where do I want to go to college? Do I want to go far from home or stay close? Large campus or a small campus, city or small town? Many students want to move away from home so that they can experience different things. But most students stay close or near to home. The most important thing is to choose a college where you feel comfortable.

<u>Type of Institution</u> – What kind of college do I want to attend? Two-year community college or four-year institution. Private or public?

Two Year College – Offers a two-year academic program of college level courses that usually leads to an associate degree. Many of these courses can be transferred to a four-year college bachelor's program. Check to see if the two-year college has an articulation agreement with any four years schools that you might be interested in.

<u>Four Year College/University</u> – Offers academic program of majors and awards a bachelor's degree. Sometimes a four-year program takes longer than four years to complete. Many four-year institutions also offer graduate programs.

<u>Private</u> – Private colleges generally have higher tuition and rely on private endowments, fundraising and tuition to meet the academic costs. They do not receive a high level of government subsidies.

<u>Public</u> – Are relatively inexpensive for state residents because they are operated and subsidized by the state where they are located.

<u>Setting</u> – College setting means college surroundings. The college setting affects the off-campus life as well as college activities and the student body. Do you care or is it in a major city, large town, small town or a rural community?

<u>Housing</u> – Where do I want to live? On campus, off campus, at home, single room or double? What about housing, do they guarantee housing for all the years that you are in attendance? Is the college close enough that you can commute from home? How far from home do you want to go to college? Do you want to commute every day or move far from home?

<u>Size</u> – Enrollment- Do I want large classes or small classes? Am I comfortable in a student body of thousands or would I prefer just hundreds? Do I want a large impersonal school or do I want to live in a closer-knit environment? Do I want to be a big fish in a little pond or a little fish in a big pond?

<u>Student Body</u> – Do I want to go to a coed school or a same sex college? What's the political and spiritual climate on campus? Are there a lot of Marxists teaching, ultra conservatives or lots of liberals? Will you find students and faculty who think the way you do?

<u>Academics</u> – Majors or course offerings. Does the college offer my major? Or if I don't know what I want to major in, does the college have a strong liberal arts curriculum that offers me lots of majors to look at? Is it an accredited school? Is academic rigor important to you? Do you want an intense academic environment or do you want to attend a college that is more laid back? Is the prestige of the school important to your family? Would it be better to have a low-grade point average from an excellent school or a great grade point average from a good school?

<u>Campus Life</u> – Sports, intramural sports, clubs, band, theater. Are athletic and recreational facilities available?

<u>Student Body</u> – Some colleges have student bodies made up of students of a particular religion, ethnicity or gender. Sometimes you prefer to be in an environment with other students with thee preferences. Is racial and ethnic identity important to you? Do you want a predominately white college or a historically black university? Is the campus diverse? Will you find people like yourself on campus?

<u>Single Sex Colleges</u> – Enrolled are students of one gender. There are not as many single sex schools today, most schools are coed.

<u>Religious Affiliated Colleges</u> – Private four-year colleges linked to a religious denomination. Most of these schools welcome students of other denominations and beliefs however. Others have strict requirements for attendance to religious services as well as a strict code of conduct.

<u>Cost</u> – Can my family afford the cost of the college? What percentage of students receive financial aid? Does the college offer scholarships? Am I eligible for federal or state based financial aid?

<u>Criteria</u> – What criteria does the college use in making admission decisions?
What is the average range of GPA, ACT or SAT scores of the majority of the students accepted? Is your family academic history important to you? Is daddy a Harvard graduate or did mom attend Spellman? Is being a legacy important to you?

Your answer to the above questions will help you to decide what is important to you as you develop your college list. You can now determine the most important factors to you in deciding which colleges to apply to.

To Be Forearmed is to be forewarned

Are you ready, did you ask yourself what you are looking for in a college? Now start doing your research to make your college list. How many schools should you select? Break it down into three categories. Which colleges are your <u>reach</u> colleges-(those that you may have a hard time getting in to) <u>reasonably attainable</u> colleges (those that you have a reasonable chance of getting accepted to and (3) <u>sure-shot</u> colleges (those that you know you'll be admitted to).

Make sure that your college list is a combination of all three categories. How many schools should you apply to? You should apply to definitely more than two colleges. Most students apply to 5 or more.

2. Create a master list of all the college deadlines for the schools that you have selected.

3. In your list of deadlines include test dates, scholarship and financial aid deadlines and housing deadlines.

4. Go on line and search college scholarships. You don't have to pay someone money to get a list of scholarships. Start with the College Board web site. You can also go to your local library and

ask the librarian to help you generate a list on line or refer you to the reference room where there are books that list scholarships.

5. If you haven't done it, you need to take the ACT or SAT exams right away. If you can take a prep class such as Kaplan or the Princeton review. These classes help you learn how to take an exam. If you don't have money ask your guidance counselor if there are any scholarships available. Look around to see if any community organizations are offering SAT or ACT prep classes. I strongly recommend that you take a prep class to give yourself a competitive edge with your SAT or ACT exam.

6. Using your college list, request college and financial aid applications from the admissions and financial aid offices that you have selected to apply to. You can also go online and request application forms from the college web sites.

7. Go to the guidance counselor's office to make sure that your high school transcripts are o.k.

8. Set up a meeting with the guidance counselor to go over your college and financial aid plans.

9. Attend college fairs and financial aid workshops.

10. Make college visits. If you haven't scheduled an interview, call the colleges that you are applying to and schedule interviews.

11. Talk to teachers, coaches etc. that know you and ask if they would write your college recommendations for you. Make sure that there are people that can write good things about you. I have read recommendation letters written for students by teachers

that had nothing good to say about them. I often wondered why a student would have someone write a recommendation letter for them that had nothing good to say about them. Give your teacher your resume to help her write more about you.

12. Write your resume. Here is a chance to begin to list all the extracurricular activities, jobs, sports etc. that you have been involved in. Putting a resume together will help you organize your thoughts so that it will be easier to complete your college applications. Sometimes it's hard to toot your own horn, but here is an opportunity to do so. Talk to your family and friends as you put the resume together. They may remember things that you have forgotten.

13. Decide if you are applying Early Decision or Early Action. This is important because deadline dates may differ. Here is the difference between Early Decision and Early Action.

<u>Early Decision</u>: If after doing your college search and you answered all the questions and you have found one college that you absolutely love and stands above all the rest, you should consider applying Early Decision. But remember if you apply Early Decision that means that if you are accepted early you are committed to enroll. And, you must make a commitment that if you are accepted you will withdraw all other applications. Check the deadline for Early Decision because its is usually in November or December of your senior year.

The advantage to you if you apply Early Decision is that if you are accepted you will discover quickly if you have been admitted and will not have the pressure that many of your friends will be experiencing waiting to hear in March or April. And, if you are not accepted you have the time to apply to other schools.

Early Action: If after doing your college search and you answered all the questions and you have found a college that you absolutely like a lot, you might consider applying Early Action. Early Action means that your application will be evaluated and a decision will be made. But the main difference between Early Decision and Early Action is that you do not have to commit to the college if you are accepted Early Action.

But remember if you apply **Early Decision** that means that if you are accepted early you are committed to enroll. Check the deadline for Early Action; usually it is in November or December of your senior year.

14. Send out your college applications to the colleges on your list. Did you narrow your list down to the three categories? Which colleges are your reach colleges-(those that you may have a hard time to get into) reasonably attainable colleges (those that you have a reasonable chance of getting accepted to and (3) sure-shot colleges (those that you know you'll be admitted to). If you have financial problems don't be afraid to talk to your guidance

counselor, they may have waivers available from some colleges for low income students who cannot afford the application fee.

Important to remember. Your college application is the first way that you represent yourself to the admissions committee. **You want to make sure that your application is clean, neat, no typos. Represent yourself well!**

What is Rolling Admission etc.?

The colleges that you apply to fall into three categories in the admissions process: Selective, Open and Rolling admissions.

<u>Selective Admissions</u>: Most of the schools that you are looking at have selective admissions. That means that their deadline dates for application fall sometime between mid-December and February. Admission decisions are mailed in late March or by early April and you have until May 1 to pay your deposit and to make your commitment. For the students who were wait-listed at the colleges, they will hear if they came off the wait- list after the May 1 deposit deadline. After the deposits are in a college knows if it has filled all of its freshman spots.

<u>Rolling Admissions</u>: If the school that you are looking at has rolling admissions that means that they will accept and reject applicants until they meet their freshman class enrollment. With a rolling admissions school you know the admission decision much early than from a selective admissions college.

<u>Open Admissions</u>: A college that states it has open admission will accept any student who meets minimal requirements, usually a high school diploma or a GED. They will admit until they fill their class. Many two-year colleges have open admissions.

After you have compiled your list of schools that meet the criteria you have selected, you can narrow your list even further by ranking your list. Which colleges are your **<u>reach</u> colleges**-(those that you may have a hard time to get into) **<u>reasonably attainable</u> colleges** (those that you have a reasonable chance of getting accepted to and (3) **<u>sure-shot</u> college**s (those that you know you'll be admitted to).

You'll have more than one favorite. You might have a first choice or even a third choice. But if you take the time to carefully make your list, you'll be happy wherever you go because you asked yourself the right questions when you were making your list of colleges to apply to.

What Not to Say during the College Interview

First look at the college catalogue. Read it. Go to the college web site and read everything that is presented about the college. Get a sense of how they present the college to prospective students. Now, make sure that you do not ask any of the obvious questions that are presented in the catalogue or the web site. For example, why would you ask about the size of the campus, the number of students enrolled etc. etc. when all of this information is included on the web site or in the college. Before you go on the interview make a list of questions that you want to ask. That will help you if you get nervous.

Here is a list of questions that you might consider, ask the same questions at each campus you visit so that you can compare:

What percentage of students graduate in four years?
How many freshmen return for their sophomore year?
What makes (college's) major/program special?
Is dorm living available for all four years?
What are some of the important campus issues?

Your interview is a way for the admission committee to put a face to your application. So, present yourself well. Be on time, dress appropriately and remember it's you chance to impress the admission committee. Let's face it; if it's between you and another applicant and you look alike academically etc. your interview may be the one thing that sets you apart. Make sure that the interview is your interview and not your parents.

And please don't forget, after your interview; don't forget to send a hand written, personal thank you note to your interviewer. This is more personal than an email and will make a favorable impression.

So, don't dress like a video vixen or in the latest hip-hop party gear. Dress like you mean it. Dress for success.

Take a Walk on the Wild Side; Explore (The Campus Visit)

The best thing that you can do is to visit the college campuses that you are thinking about applying to. Take a walk on campus, explore. And, the earlier the better. This is one way to pare down your college selection list. If the campus doesn't feel right to you, it's not the right place for you no matter how selective or prestigious it is. You want to attend a college where you will prosper.

And while you are there, sit in on a class, talk to students. Ask them some of the questions that you might be intimidated to ask the admissions counselor. While on the campus talk to currently enrolled students and ask some of the following questions:

What is the best thing about the college and the worst thing?
Who really teaches the classes, the teaching assistants or the full professors?
What's fun to do on campus?
Are there good advisors when you can't decide you're major?
Do you have to have a car on campus?

Now ask yourself some questions. Can you see yourself on the campus for two years, four years? Are currently enrolled students the type of people that you would like to be with for the next few years? What are the professors like? What is the campus culture? And most importantly, make sure that you don't visit during exam week when the campus is shut down.

Visiting classes is a must. Were the students and faculty approachable? Who was teaching, was it really senior professors or graduate students? Think about it, you are spending a lot of money to go to college, so be a good consumer. Find the right college fit for you. Not the fit for a good friend

Deadly/Killer Mistakes You Can Make When Applying to College

Over the years I have seen high school students sabotage their chances of getting into college because they don't realize how important it is to be on their game. They rush through the application, don't take the time to read the application thoroughly and hurt their chances of being considered legitimately. Listed below are a few things to think about as you are developing your strategy.

Applying to a College Sight Unseen

Sure, you can find out about colleges by going on the web, reading catalogs and brochures and or talking to alumni. But there is nothing like seeing the campus yourself. When you visit a campus, you get a feel for the campus community. Talking to currently enrolled students, sitting in classes and just walking on campus gives you a sense of whether or not you will fit in. You definitely want to be at a college that you feel comfortable attending. Because, if you apply to a college, get accepted and enroll without seeing it, you may find out that it was the wrong fit for you. Then you have to start the process all over again and look for the college to transfer to where you feel comfortable. I know that you don't want to do that right?

I did that. I applied to a college because the college recruiter was cute. Then I enrolled in the college sight unseen. I never visited campus until freshman registration. You should have seen my face when we pulled up on campus and I found that I was in the middle of nowhere and the nowhere was acres and acres of corn fields. There wasn't a mall, corner store or a place to go to or nothing to do unless you had a car. And if you didn't have a car, forget about it. There was no where to shop, no where to escape to. Not even a movie theater. Sometimes you need a break from campus life.

Thinking You Can't Afford a College so You Don't Apply.

Just because the college is expensive doesn't mean that you can't afford it. There is a big difference between the sticker price (the cost of the college) and what you actually pay. Over 66% of all students who attend college receive some form of financial aid to assist them with the cost of college. So, don't make the mistake of saying that you can't afford a college because of the price tag and you don't apply. You never if a school is affordable unless you try.

Over Embellishing Your College Application. Tell the Truth

Please don't make up information on your college application. If the admissions committee finds out that you didn't tell the truth on your application it could be deadly to your admission to that school. Honesty is the best policy. Plus, you never know who people know and with the Internet the world is getting smaller and smaller. So, don't tell them that you are a child prodigy in music and can't play a note.

I know of a student who said that their father was dead on their financial aid application hoping that they would get money from financial aid and then listed their father's address on the admission application. Unfortunately, for the student, he never realized that the admissions office and the financial aid office communicate with each other. On top of that, it's against the law to give misleading or false information on your FAFSA (Free Application for Federal Student Aid). Don't do it!

Mailing in a Messy Application

Your college application may be the first time the admission committee meets you. So, you want to put your best foot forward. Believe it or not, your application represents you. So, if you submit an application that is messy, ridden with spelling errors, white out ink and crossed through words, you don't represent yourself well. Your mother was right, neatness counts. Did you know that over 90% of all college applications submitted are neat, clean and spell checked? Yes, you want to make an impression on the admission committee, but you want to make the right impression. Your application is your future, take it seriously. This is one time when a do-over counts.

Blowing the Deadline: Does It Really Matter?

Don't put yourself in the situation where you have to plead with the admissions officer to accept your application late. Thousands of students have applied to the college by the deadline date. You want to be sure that you are one of them. That's why it's important to be organized. With limited acceptance spaces, your lateness to be the reason why your college application was rejected. The early bird always gets the worm.

If it's Not an Ivy You Don't Apply

Don't choose a school only because it's prestigious. Choose it because it's the right college for you. Of course, a college with an excellent reputation can help you with your career goals. Look at the number of United States Presidents and Congresspersons who attended prestigious colleges. Always remember that selective colleges are just that, selective.

Blowing Off College Recommendations

Maybe you didn't know it, but your recommendation letters are very important in the college admission process. Your recommendation letter presents information to the admission committee that may not be seen in your application. For example, suppose you were a late bloomer and didn't come into you own academically until your junior and senior years. Maybe your 9th grade grades weren't stronger and the 10th grade grades were better but not stellar. If the admissions committee is trying to understand what may have happened and/or may be deciding between accepting and rejecting you, the committee may look closer at your recommendation letters. Your recommendation letter might explain that you were sick your sophomore year or something traumatic happened in your family that affected you. Or they might just say that you are a late bloomer. Nevertheless, you want someone to write your recommendation letters who likes you and has good things to say about you.

I remember looking at a few applicants' recommendation letters where I wondered why they choose a particular individual to write one for them. It was clear that the recommender was not a fan of the student. Sometimes it's not what they but how they say it or what they didn't say.

Putting Your Mother in Charge of Your College Application

Don't leave your college application in the hands of someone else, even your mother. It's easy to have your parents complete your application or even to hire a college coach to do it for you. But that won't help you as much as if you do it yourself. Sure, your parents and/or college coach can advise you. They will even help you make some important decisions. But the bottom line is that they can't pick the college that will be the perfect fit for you. Only you know what that will be. The decisions that you make now will affect the rest of your life. So, don't put someone else in charge of your destiny.

Are You in or Are You Out? - Getting In

Now we are in one of the most important sections of this book. How to get into college. What does the admission committee look at in making the decision to accept or reject you? What is the most important thing that the admissions committee looks at?

You're High School Record

It all starts and begins with your high school record. Every school wants to enroll the best students. So, if your high school transcripts covered with lots of as, the more the better. You know already that Cs and Ds aren't favorable to you. They also want to see how you challenged yourself academically. Did you take the AP and Honors courses? Did you Receive the IB (International Baccalaureate)? AP, Honors and IB all look good on your high school transcript; because the admissions committee knows that you took a rigorous curriculum.

The committee also looks to see if you took an academic core curriculum: English, Math, Science, Social Studies and a Foreign Language. Most schools would like to see at least four years of classes in the core, you definitely need three years.

What if you got a B instead of an A in an AP class? The admissions committee respects that B when they can see that you stretched yourself to get that B rather than settling for a class where you could get the A.

What If Your High School Doesn't Have AP or Honors Classes?

College admissions officers know that all schools are not equal. Let's face it, some schools offer AP, Honors and IB classes and other do not. When the admissions committee evaluates your high school transcript they also look at the courses that are being offered at your school. They want to see what you did with the academic opportunity that was before you. Did you challenge yourself or take the easy way out, taking easy classes to maintain a high GPA?

Supposed you Started off Slow in High School

Maybe you were a late bloomer, or something happened where you couldn't get it together in 9th grade. Maybe even 10th grade wasn't that great either. The most important thing to the admissions committee is that your grades kept climbing. Each term they saw growth in the academic record. As you move through high school guidance counselors want to see steady growth.

The Dreaded Test Scores: How Much Do They Count

Let's face it, your test scores do count even though there are a few colleges that don't require it. When you review the college applications make sure that you check to see which test scores are required. Colleges use your test scores for placement purposes. They want to see how you will fit in with the other students enrolled at the college. If you can't afford to take the test ask your guidance counselor for a fee waiver. If you need disability accommodations request them.

But the good news is that you have a better chance of getting higher test scores thanks to the excellent SAT/ACT prep classes that are now being offered by Princeton Review, Kaplan etc. to help you improve your scores. These courses will help relieve your test anxiety because they offer samples practice tests to take. These tests will be used to evaluate your strengths and weaknesses so that you can develop a strategy for test taking.

One of the things to look at as you compare your scores to other students is to look at the range of SAT or ACT scores of the accepted students. This will give you an opportunity to see how your scores compare to the other students.

If you haven't taken your test yet here are some tips:

If you missed the registration deadlines, apply to take the test stand-by.

Drive by the test location before the test day to make sure that you know where it is and how long it will take to get there.
Get a good night's sleep before the test.
Make sure that your name is written and spelled the same on your test papers and your college applications.
Read all the instructions before starting. You will save time in the end.

The College Essay

Let's face it; your college essay is important. If it is done poorly, your essay presentation is messy with lots of errors, typos and misspelled words, the admissions committee is not going to take you seriously. This may be the only way that you can tell the admissions committee more about you. And if you don't take it seriously, why should they. Remember the content is more important than the length of the essay. It's time to think for yourself

Plus, there is so much information on the web and tins of book to help you:
www.essayedge.com
www.personalessay.com
www.collegeboard.com
How to Write a Winning College Essay by Harold Bauld
The College Application Essay by Sarah Myers McGinty

I' m Special: I'm Brilliant, A Jock, or Disabled

Merit Scholarship

Merit money is any money that is given and not based on need. Merit scholarships come in many forms. It could be academic merit, athletic merit (discussed below), musical merit, dramatic merit, artistic merit or geographic merit. Merit money is used to attract the best and the brightest students that they want. Just be sure that you ask the college about your merit scholarship:
Is it offered for all the years that you are enrolled in the college? What do you have to do to maintain the scholarship?

For example, suppose you are offered an academic scholarship and you have to maintain a certain grade point average. What happens to your scholarship if your average changes. They requite a 3.5 GPA and you have a 3.0 GPA. Do you automatically loose your scholarship or do you get the opportunity to improve it the next academic term?
Or maybe you have a musical scholarship, what happens if you stop playing in the band?

All of the above questions are important. If you don't ask you don't know what your responsibility is a student. If the scholarship is discontinued, you have to find a way to cover it yourself.

<u>Athletic Scholarships</u>

Before signing the letter or intent or collecting an athletic scholarship offer, please make sure that you understand what the requirements of the scholarship are. An athletic scholarship means that you have to play the sport you were recruited for. But ask yourself an important question, what happens if you get injured and can't play any longer, can you still keep your scholarship? What happens if you are cut from the team? Although sports are important you want the degree. Don't forget to ask about graduation rates for student athletes.

While on campus talk to some of the student athletes. Ask about how they manage classes and practice, absences from classes while traveling, what kind of tutoring is available.

There are many other considerations to make: Do you want to go to a Division I or a Division III school. For information about college scholarships and the responsibilities of a student athlete the NCAA website includes a "Guide for the College Bound Student Athlete". Your college guidance counselor may also have a copy.

<u>www.ncaa.org</u>

Students with Disabilities or Special Needs

The number of first-time college students with disabilities has significantly increased over the past thirty years. And, because of Section 504 of the Rehabilitation Act of 1973 all institutions that receive federal funds must provide accommodations for students with disabilities. The Americans with Disabilities Act of 1990 also provides guidelines for colleges about accessible classrooms, books on tapes, readers, interpreters, note takers, tutors, extended time exams etc. When visiting a campus make sure that you contact the student affairs office that deals with students with disabilities. If you can meet with a student with a similar disability while on campus it will be very helpful. Listed below is a list of web sites and books that can help you find the right college to meet your needs:

Association of Higher Education and Disability
www.ahead.org

National Council on Assisted Living
ncil@ncil.org

The National Clearinghouse on Postsecondary Education for Individuals with Disabilities contains a list of programs across the country.
www.heath.gwu.edu

"Peterson's Colleges with Programs for Students with Learning Disabilities or Attention Deficit Disorders", by Charles Mangrum and Stephen Strichart.

Deposits (What if You Haven't Heard from Every College Yet)

The deposit request is important. What it means is that your cash deposit guarantees your spot and is evidence that you are serious about enrolling in the college. But sometimes Colleges request deposits before you have heard from all the colleges that you have applied to. That puts you in quite a dilemma. My suggestion is that you secure your spot in at least one of the early colleges that accepted you so that you have a spot for the fall. You never know what will happen with the rest of the applications and you don't want to go bust.

And to make you and your parents feel better, call the admissions office and ask if your deposit is refundable. Most colleges understand this and will refund your acceptance deposit if you change your mind. Then, if you get a better offer later when all the acceptances are in you can ask for the refund. The main and most important thing is to cover yourself with your deposit by the college deadline date. College know that students change their minds when better offers come in.

The Dreaded Wait List

You may be disappointed that you were placed on the college wait list from the one of your colleges that you applied to. Being on the college wait list means that if a space opens up to fill a freshman spot, a student from the wait list will be selected. But if you don't return the card and say so that you want to stay on the waitlist, you won't have a shot. So, why not, send back the card. Especially, if you like the school and would still enroll if you come off the wait list, you have nothing to lose. Every year there are students who come off the wait list because the college did not enroll their class. Fill out the wait list card!

Deferring Admission

Sometimes you might want to defer your acceptance for a year and travel abroad, work or simply stay home. Check with the college to see what arrangements you must make in order to defer or if you must reapply.

I've Got Senioritis

Don't get it. You don't want it. Senioritis is when you stop working in your senior year once the college acceptance letters are out. Your grades plummet but you don't care because you are in, you have several college acceptances under your belt. Resist, fight it, do whatever you have to stay on course. You don't want senioritis. It's harmful to your health. Did you know that colleges do look at and require your final high school senior year transcript? And, did you know that colleges have the right to rescind your college acceptance based on the final transcript? Beware of seniors with senioritis, it's contagious and could be harmful to your college acceptance.

COVID

Many things have changed in the college environment since the COVID pandemic. Check with the Office of Student Admissions to verify what vaccinations are needed prior to enrollment and COVID policies that are in place.

Final Words

Your future is in your hands. Right now, you have the opportunity and power to successfully survive the college admission process. It's all in your hands but you have to work hard. You have to ask questions, ask for help and make some life choices. But, if you follow the steps that I have given you, you will learn how to choose a college, what a college looks for in the college application and what you can do as a senior to guarantee your admissions.

About the Author:

Deborah Battle Pointer was the former Associate Dean of Admissions and Financial Aid at Cornell University, former Director of Admissions at the Columbia University School of Engineering and former Director of Financial Aid at Columbia College of Columbia University. She has also served as the Director of Financial Aid at SUNY Downstate Medical Center serving undergraduates and medical students and now is a Fellowship Coordinator for physicians. While living in Ithaca, New York she was elected to the Ithaca School Board where she served two terms. Ms. Pointer has authored several magazine articles on financing a college education and has worked on a series of videotapes on financial aid for students. The videotapes aired on the Public Broadcasting television stations in the New York tri-state area. For many years she was a consultant to ESPN on selecting the High School Athlete of the Year.

Deborah Pointer is a published poet, novelist and television producer. She received a Peabody Award for excellence in television and is co-founder and Executive Producer of "Russell Simmons Def Poetry Jam" on the HBO Network.

You're In!

9 798376 020968